Summer Drinks

A collection of delicious non-alcoholic beverages

With recipes from Canada's best cafés and restaurants

Elizabeth Feltham

Formac Publishing Company Limited
Halifax

Formac Publishing Company Limited
acknowledges the support of the Cultural Affairs
Section, Nova Scotia Department of Tourism and
Culture. We acknowledge the support of the
Government of Canada through the Book
Publishing Industry Development Program (BPIDP)
for our publishing activities.

**National Library of Canada Cataloguing in
Publication Data**

Feltham, Elizabeth
    Summer drinks : a collection of delicious non-
alcoholic beverages, with recipes from Canada's
best cafés and restaurants / by Elizabeth Feltham.

Includes index.

ISBN 0-88780-620-1

    1. Non-alcoholic beverages. I. Title.

TX815.F44 2004   641.8'75   C2004-900552-9

Printed and bound in China

Photo Credits

*Julian Beveridge: pages 1, 4-5, 8-9, 11, 12, 13,
14,15, 17, 18-19, 20, 24, 26, 33, 34, 38, 42, 43.,
49, 57, 61, 64, 69, 70, 71, 72, 73, 76, 78,
81 (top), 84, 85, 93, 95*

*Janet Kimber: front cover, pages 2-3, 6, 7, 10, 16,
22, 23, 25, 28, 29, 30-31, 32, 35, 36, 39, 40-41,
44, 46, 47, 50, 51, 53, 54, 59, 60, 68, 74, 77,
80, 82, 86, 87, 88-9, 91, 94*

Dedication

To Sue Feltham, the bravest woman I know.

— E.F.

Formac Publishing Company Limited
5502 Atlantic Street
Halifax, Nova Scotia
B3H 1G4
www.formac.ca

Contents

Acknowledgements

The author and publisher acknowledge the
following in assisting the production of this book.
Mills Brothers, Halifax, Vision Food Systems;
Paderno Factory Store; Jean Perry/On Foot
Glassworks; Ambience Home Accents; Lilian
Chapman, for glassware
James MacDougall of La Perla for food styling
All the participating chefs and restaurant owners
for recipes. Manohar Ahir for making the author
cups of wonderful tea; and Chef Raj Gupta for
recipes and continuing support.

Introduction

What better way to drink in summer's gentle touch than with home-made lemonade, or brewed iced tea! This collection of drinks recipes is especially for lazy afternoons in a hammock,

get-togethers on the patio and romantic dinners on a sultry August evening.

Classic summer drinks have been enjoyed for generations, and are still wonderfully appealing. In these pages you'll find some intriguing thirst quenchers — raspberry vinegar, for instance, which deserves a revival, and homemade ginger beer, also making a come-

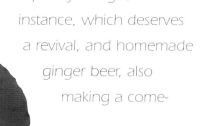

back. You can also indulge in the recent enthusiasm for fresh local ingredients, steering away from manufactured products, and you can create delicious fresh fruit blends. The preference of many adults for non-alcoholic summer drinks has encouraged chefs and bartenders in many of Canada's finest restaurants towards chic healthy beverages. This book was inspired by their success and they have generously contributed their most imaginative ideas in drinks for use here.

Starting with the experts' recipes and their suggestions for garnishes, we have recreated their drinks and photographed them so you can see how attractive they are to the eye. As to their appeal to your tastebuds, you'll have to try them out!

This book is organized into eight sections, beginning with tall drinks, such as variations on lemonade and punch, as well as the Mexican favourite Agua Fresca and a non-alcoholic Sangria.

Bring out your cocktail shaker for the

very sophisticated 'mocktails,' including Strawberry Daiquiri, Quattrini and Rhubarb Colada.

And for pure vitamins turn to the Sips of Sunshine featuring fruit and vegetable juices. Serve up the iced tea and iced coffee selections in the Cool Cuppa section and you will win hands down the debate as to whether a hot beverage is preferable to a cool one on a stifling summer's day.

Lassi is a popular yogurt drink in India. In this book we bring you variations on lassi along with some traditional fruit smoothies. For party time you need drinks that are dazzling – in looks and taste. All you need is some funky glasses and straws and serve up Lava Flow or Jungle Juice. Finally we offer some creamy delights such as Sorbetto al Limone, Chocolate Monkey and Double Blueberry Malt, all of which can double as dessert.

Many of these drinks call for crushed ice and chilled glasses. It is possible to crush ice in a good blender, but better to either buy it already crushed or break up larger blocks before putting them in the blender. Put the blocks in a plastic bag and smash them with a rolling pin or similar blunt, heavy tool.

Juicers, blenders and drink mixers are also called for in these recipes, which really makes it easy to whip up a batch of fresh fruit drinks. Nevertheless, almost all of these treats could be made with a food mill, a cocktail shaker and a whisk.

Citrus Thirst Quenchers

Lemonades, Limeades, Orangeades

There's nothing quite so delicious as a tall glass of ice-cold lemonade on a hot summer's day. Since one glass of lemonade is never enough, these recipes all serve at least four glasses.

Left: Orangeade, Limeade, Lemonade

GREEN LAKE GUZZLER

EDGEWATER LODGE, WHISTLER, BC

This is a tart thirst quencher that lives up to the name "guzzler" — on a hot summer day you won't be able to drink it fast enough! For the freshest, healthiest apple juice, buy organic apples and use a juicer. A centrifugal juicer works well — think of a washing machine in the spin cycle. A basket with a grater whirls the fruit around, pushing the juice through the front of the machine and keeping the peel and pulp against the walls of the basket.

2 cups (500 ml) fresh lime juice
4 cups (1 L) apple juice
3 cups (750 ml) soda water
mint leaves for garnish

Combine lime juice, apple juice and soda water in large pitcher, stir.

Serve in glasses rimmed with sugar and garnish drink with mint leaf

serves 12 juice glasses

OLD-FASHIONED LEMONADE

The signature drink of summer, this lemonade is just tart enough to quench your thirst without too much pucker.

4 cups (1 L) water
1 cup (250mL) sugar
1 cup (250 ml) lemon juice (6 lemons)
2 oranges, juiced
zest of 2 oranges

In medium saucepan, combine water and sugar. Bring to boil and stir until sugar dissolves. Let cool. Add lemon juice, orange juice and orange zest. Cover and let stand 1 hour, then strain and refrigerate. Serve chilled.

For pink lemonade, add a tablespoon of raspberry or strawberry syrup.

serves 4 tall glasses

LEMON-GRASS GINGER LEMONADE

DUNES RESORT, BRACKLEY BEACH, PEI

A new twist on the old favourite — the lemon grass is subtle, exotic flavour and ginger's heat should make this one of your new favourites. The amounts of sugar and ginger can be adjusted for personal taste.

1 cup (250 ml) sugar
2-4 stalks lemon grass,* sliced
1 piece (2" or about a thumb length) ginger, peeled and sliced
4 cups (1 L) water
3 lemons, juiced (about 90 ml)
2 limes, juiced (about 60 ml)
Pinch of sea salt
2 cups (500 ml) ice

In medium saucepan, combine sugar, lemongrass, ginger and water and bring to boil. Simmer for 20 minutes. Remove from heat and let sit for 1 hour to steep and develop flavour. Strain into a pitcher. Add lemon juice, lime juice, salt and ice.

* When choosing lemon grass, look for plump lower stalks. This is the only part you'll use for this drink.

serves 4 tall glasses

Left: Lemon-grass Ginger Lemonade

LIVELY LIMEADE

For a tangy twist on the more traditional lemonade, try this lively libation.

4 cups (1L) water
3/4 cups (175 ml) sugar
8 limes, juiced (3/4 cup / 175 ml)

In medium saucepan, combine water and sugar. Bring to boil and stir until sugar dissolves. Let cool. Stir in lime juice. Refrigerate and serve chilled.

serves 4 tall glasses

When buying limes for juicing, look for well rounded fruits that feel heavy for their size. A little browning on the skin won't affect flavour, but avoid shrivelled or hard limes.

PLOUGHMAN'S COOLER

OPA!, HALIFAX, NS

This recipe was handed down from Chef Joseph's father and grandfather. "In those days" notes Chef Joseph "there was no Coca Cola." It's an unusual drink, but well-suited for hot summer days especially when doing outside work like gardening.

1 cup (250 ml) seedless raisins
4 cups (1 L) cold water
Rind of 1/2 orange, chopped
Rind of 1/2 lemon, chopped
Pine nuts, for garnish

In large glass container, mix raisins, water, orange and lemon rind. Refrigerate overnight. Strain and serve chilled. Garnish with pine nuts.

serves 4 water glasses

To get the most juice from your lemons, let them come to room temperature before juicing. For a really old-fashioned lemonade or orangeade experience, you must forgo an electric citrus juicer in favour of a wooden reamer. Slice the fruit in half. Insert the tip of the reamer and hold the fruit over a bowl while you squeeze and ream.

LEMON-GRASS LEMONADE

URBAN HERB, BELLEVILLE, ON

The Urban Herb is located in one of the oldest buildings in Belleville. Tim Hennig (with wife Sharon) offer an eclectic menu, and this lemon grass lemonade is a worldly twist on an old-fashioned staple.

8 cups (2 L) water
1/2 cup (125 ml) chopped ginger
3 stalks lemon grass, chopped
6 dried/3 fresh Kaffir lime leaves
2 lemons, quartered
2 limes, quartered
Pinch salt
1/2 cup sugar

In medium saucepan, combine water, ginger, lemon grass, lime leaves, lemons and limes. Bring to boil, then reduce to simmer for about 1 hour. When all ingredients sink to bottom, mixture is ready. Strain the loose ingredients, being sure to squeeze all liquid out. Add salt, then add sugar a little at a time until desired sweetness is achieved.

Chill and serve.

serves 8 tall glasses

AWESOME ORANGEADE

Nothing beats the taste of fresh-squeezed orange juice. For a different looking orangeade, try blood oranges. These red-fleshed oranges, typically available throughout Canada in spring and early summer, are every bit as juicy and vitamin-C packed as their more conventional cousins.

1 cup (250 ml) water
1 cup (250 ml) sugar
1 orange rind, zested
1 lemon rind, zested
1/4 cup (50 ml) fresh-squeezed lemon juice
2 cups (500 ml) fresh-squeezed orange juice
3 cups (750 ml) ice water

In medium saucepan, combine water and sugar. Bring to boil and stir until sugar dissolves. Add orange and lemon zest. Boil gently until mixture thinly coats the back of a spoon, about ten minutes. Strain and cool. In container, combine cooled syrup, lemon juice, orange juice and ice water. Stir. Refrigerate and serve chilled.

serves 6 tall glasses

Plentiful
Punch

...and Sparkling Cordials

A generous bowl of chilled punch is a great way to
welcome guests to a patio get-together. Recipes for
favourites, like Sangria, and old traditionals, such as
Rhubarb Punch, are presented here, along with
instructions for home-made root beer and ginger beer.

Left: Agua Fresca

GINGER PUNCH

DUNDEE ARMS INN,
MABOU, NS

This tart punch packs quite the ginger kick — you can adjust the amount of ginger as you prefer. If preserved ginger is unavailable, you may substitute fresh, measure for measure.

4 cups (1 L) water
1 cup (250 ml) sugar
1/2 cup (125 ml) chopped
preserved ginger
1/2 cup (125 ml) pineapple
juice
1/2 cup (125 ml) lemon juice
1/2 cup (125ml) orange juice
2 cups (500 ml) soda water (or
to taste)

In large pot, boil water, sugar and ginger slowly for 15 minutes. Add pineapple, lemon and orange juices, stir and chill. Dilute to desired taste with soda water.

serves 8 tall glasses

LANGDON HALL PUNCH

LANGDON HALL, CAMBRIDGE, ON

Cranberries and apples are not summer fruit but cider and frozen cranberry juice are readily available all year round to make this healthy thirst quencher.

4 cups (1L) cranberry juice
2 cups (500 ml) sparkling apple cider, non-alcoholized
3 cups (750 ml) soda water
1/2 cup (125 ml) fresh or frozen whole cranberries, for ice cubes

Pour cranberry juice, sparkling apple cider and soda water over ice cubes into a large punch bowl.

Serve with ice cubes in which whole cranberries have been frozen. Fill up your ice cube trays, then drop a cranberry or two into each section of the tray before freezing.

serves 12 punch cups

GINGER BEER

Ginger beer is an excellent thirst quencher but definitely an acquired taste. A staple in warm climates like Jamaica, it's the forerunner of more commercial, sweeter, ginger ale.

*2 oz (30 ml) fresh ginger,
    minced
2 lemons, sliced
1 lime, sliced
1 tsp (5 ml) cream of tartar
1 lb (450 g) sugar
1 gallon (4 L) boiling water
1 tsp (5 ml) dry yeast*

In large container, such as a 2-gallon (8 L) jug, combine ginger, lemon, lime, cream of tartar and sugar. Pour in boiling water and stir. Let sit until mixture is just warm, then stir in yeast. Tightly cover jug and let sit for 24 hours. Strain, chill and serve.

serves 10 beer mugs

HOMEMADE ROOT BEER

You can make just about any soda at home following the same basic steps as this root beer recipe. Flavour extracts, which today, substitute for the "real root" such as sarsaparilla or sassafras, are available at most home brewing stores. Just remember to watch for the carbonation — some of these bottles have more power than popping champagne!

1 tsp (5 ml) dry yeast
1/2 cup (125 ml) warm water
16 cups (4 L) hot water
2 cups (500 ml) sugar
4 tsp (20 ml) root beer extract

Dissolve yeast in 1/2 cup (125 ml) warm water and let stand 5 minutes. In 4 cups (1 L) of the hot water, dissolve sugar. In 1-gallon (4 L) jug, combine yeast and sugar water, stir in root beer extract. Add remaining hot water and stir until ingredients are well combined. Tightly cover jug and let sit in sun for 4 hours. Remove from sun and let sit overnight, or for 8 hours. Refrigerate and serve chilled in frosted mugs.

serves 10 beer mugs

FIRE-EATER

ACTON'S GRILL AND CAFÉ, WOLFVILLE, NS

Apple juice tames the heat of the ginger beer in this tangy blend. Use the homemade ginger beer (p. 22) and fresh pressed apple juice for an authentic home 'brew'.

1/2 cup (125 ml) apple juice
1/2 cup (125 ml) ginger beer

Combine apple juice and ginger beer and serve over ice.

serves 1 tall glass

AGUA FRESCA

Agua Fresca is the national fruit punch of Mexico and is traditionally served from glass barrel-shaped containers.

3 cups (750 ml) chopped fresh fruit (any kind may be used, but common choices include cantaloupe, watermelon and strawberries)
8 cups (2 L) water
3/4 (175 ml) cup sugar
1/4 cup 50 ml) fresh lemon juice

In blender, add fruit and 3 cups (750 ml) of water. Purée until smooth, then strain through sieve. Add rest of water, sugar and lemon juice. Stir and serve.

serves 8 large margarita glasses

You can adjust the amount of sugar in recipes for fresh fruit drinks according to taste and the sweetness of the fruit.

RHUBARB PUNCH

MARSHLANDS INN, SACKVILLE, NB

Rhubarb punch is a traditional offering at Marshlands Inn, made from their home-grown rhubarb. A small glass of the tart punch is refreshing accompaniment to a light summer supper.

For syrup
10 lbs (4.5 kg) rhubarb cut in short lengths
8 cups (2 L) sugar
water to cover
For drink
6 to 8 cups (1 1/2 to 2 L) soda water

Place rhubarb in pot, add sugar and pour in water until rhubarb is just covered. Cook over medium heat until rhubarb is tender, about 10 to 15 minutes. Strain through fine wire mesh strainer into bowl and refrigerate liquid until cold. Yield should be 6 to 8 (1 1/2 to 2 L) cups.

To make punch, mix equal amounts of rhubarb syrup and soda water. The syrup may be frozen in 1 cup containers to make a couple of glasses at a time, or used immediately to make a large bowl of punch.

Yields 6-8 cups of syrup for 12–16 cups (1.1/2 L–2 L syrup for 3-4 L punch)

Left: Rhubarb Punch

PAPAYA PINEAPPLE COCONUT PUNCH

CASINO NOVA SCOTIA AND HOTEL, HALIFAX, NS

At the first sip of this exotic punch you will be transported from your backyard to a tropical island.

1 Thai coconut
2 tbsp (30 ml) freshly grated coconut
2 tbsp (30 ml) fresh papaya
2 cups (500 ml) pineapple juice
4 tsp (20 ml) sugar
4 ice cubes

Cut the top off the coconut, and drain the liquid into a bowl. Reserve one cup of coconut water and set aside. Scrape the coconut meat from the top of the shell and grate two tablespoons. In blender, combine grated coconut, papaya, pineapple juice, coconut milk, sugar, and ice cubes. Serve immediately in tall glasses with straws and umbrellas.

serves 4 tall glasses

Thai coconut can be found in Asian markets and can be substituted with other fresh coconuts. Purchase two or three additional coconuts and use the half-shells to serve this tropical drink.

SANGRIA

CHIVES BISTRO, HALIFAX, NS

Sangria, that classic Spanish punch, is as much about being yourself as it's about sticking to a recipe. This version is a great foundation, but don't hesitate to experiment with seasonal fruits and various de-alcoholized wines. Sangria made with white wine is called "sangria blanco," and it's somewhat lighter in taste.

For syrup:
1 cup (250 ml) water
1 cup (250 ml) white sugar
2 cinnamon sticks
3 whole cloves
2 orange rinds, zested
1 lemon rind, zested

For drink:
1 cup (250 ml) syrup
4 cups (1 L) alcohol-free cabernet
2 cups (500 ml) orange juice
1 cup (250 ml) ginger ale
1 peach, sliced
1 orange, sliced
1 lemon, sliced
2 cups (500 ml) sliced strawberries
sliced fruit, for garnish

To make the syrup: Bring water to boil, stir in sugar and dissolve. Add cinnamon sticks, cloves, orange and lemon zest. Simmer for 5 minutes, then remove from heat and let steep 1 hour. After syrup has steeped, strain into mixing bowl. Add de-alcoholized wine, orange juice, ginger ale, peach, orange, lemon and strawberry slices. Chill overnight in covered container.

Serve from a glass pitcher into wine glasses, with fruit slices.

serves 8 wineglasses

Right: Sangria

Chic Mocktails

Non-Martini, Daiquiri and Colada

Gone are the days when Shirley Temples and Virgin Caesars were on the children's menu only. Mocktails have come of age, and are as deliciously diverse as their spirited cousins. These chic mocktails are both old favourites as well as innovative indulgences.

Left: Strawberry Colada

DEVLIN'S MOJITO

DEVLIN'S COUNTRY BISTRO, MOUNT PLEASANT, ON

Lemons and limes make this light, bubbly drink a most refreshing choice for afternoon garden parties in the dog days of summer.

1 cup (250 ml) soda water
1 tbsp (15 ml) lemon juice
2 tbsp (30 ml) lime juice
1/2 tsp (2 ml) fresh chopped mint

In highball glass, combine soda water, lemon and lime juices and chopped mint. Stir and serve, garnished with a wedge of lime.

serves 1 tall glass

PUSSYFOOT COCKTAIL

ACTON'S GRILL AND CAFÉ, WOLFVILLE, NS

A delightful pre-dinner mocktail of blended citrus juices tamed with grenadine.

1/4 cup (50 ml) crushed ice
1/2 tsp (2 ml) grenadine
6 tbsp (90 ml) orange juice
1 tbsp (15 ml) lemon juice
3 tbsp (45 ml) lime juice
6 tbsp (90 ml) soda water
citrus wedges, for garnish

Put ice in highball glass. Pour in grenadine, orange, lemon and lime juices and soda water.

Serve in a glass and garnish with a maraschino cherry and a slice of lemon.

serves 1 martini glass

Right: Pussyfoot Cocktail

CAPE SMOKEY MOUNTAIN BERRY DAIQUIRI

CASTLE ROCK INN, INGONISH, NS

According to the McLennans, owners of the
Castle Rock Inn, a forest fire on Smokey Mountain
thirty years ago lead to an abundance of wild
blueberries in the area. This delicious pre-dinner
drink uses local berries to full advantage.

1/2 cup (125 ml) fresh blueberries
1 cup (500 ml) fresh cranberry juice
1/2 tsp (2 ml) lemon juice
3 tbsp (45 ml) raw sugar
1 cup (500 ml) crushed ice
1/2 cup (125 ml) sugar, 6 to 8 whole blueberries
*   and 2 slices lemon, for garnish*

Add blueberries, cranberry and lemon juices, raw
sugar and crushed ice to blender. Process 10 to
20 seconds, pour and serve.

Rim martini or daiquiri
glasses with sugar,
garnish with lemon
slices and whole
berries.

**serves 2 large wine
glasses**

Left: Cape Smokey Mountain Berry Daiquiri

STRAWBERRY DAIQUIRI

KIELY INN AND RESTAURANT, NIAGARA-ON-THE-LAKE, ON

There's no better way to drink in the strawberry season than this elegant mocktail.

1/2 cup (125 ml) crushed ice
3 fresh strawberries
2 tbsp (30 ml) lime juice
6 tbsp (90 ml) orange juice
2 tbsp (30 ml) pineapple juice

In blender, add crushed ice, strawberries, lime, orange and pineapple juices. Process 10 to 15 seconds, serve.

serves 1 medium goblet

RHUBARB COLADA

THE OTHER BROTHER'S RESTAURANT & PATIO, GUELPH, ON

Tired of the predictable? The Rhubarb Colada is an innovative alternative.

4 tbsp (60 ml) rhubarb juice (p. 27)
2 tbsp (30 ml) coconut bar syrup
2 tbsp (30 ml) pineapple juice
1/2 tsp (2 ml) lime juice
2 tbsp (30 ml) 10% cream

In cocktail shaker with plenty of ice, add rhubarb juice, coconut bar syrup, pineapple juice, lime juice and cream. Shake well and serve.

serves 1 martini glass

SILVER SHADOW

ACTON'S GRILL AND CAFÉ, WOLFVILLE, NS

Served in a large martini glass and garnished with a leaf of lemon verbena or basil, the Silver Shadow makes a very elegant evening drink.

1/2 cup (125 ml) crushed ice
2 tbsp (30 ml) simple syrup*
1/4 cup (50 ml) lime cordial
3/4 cup (175 ml) grapefruit juice

Put ice in glass, add simple syrup, lime cordial and grapefruit juice. Stir.

*Simple syrup, or bar syrup, is made by dissolving equal parts sugar in equal parts boiling water. The syrup is then chilled and used for drink making, to avoid the grittiness of sugar being stirred into cold liquid.

serves 1 tall glass

BROKEN HEART

BARTLETT LODGE, ALGONQUIN PARK, ON.

With a name like "Broken Heart," this sounds like a drink for a sad occasion, but actually, it's a delicious frothy mocktail suitable at any time.

6 cherries, pitted
1 cup (250 ml) fruit punch
1/4 cup (50 ml) sugar
1/2 cup (125 ml) whipped cream
1 cup (250 ml) soda water
1 tbsp (15 ml) grenadine

Cover cherries with fruit punch and 1/8 cup sugar, let stand 15 minutes then remove cherries and set aside. Whip cream with remaining 1/8 cup sugar and set aside. Pour soda water into two tall glasses, then slowly pour in fruit punch, forming layers.

Top with whipped cream, drizzle grenadine into glasses and garnish with reserved cherries.

serves 2 tall glasses

STRAWBERRY COLADA

FERN RESORT, ORILLIA, ON

Refreshing and substantial, this colada is made for lazy afternoons beside the pool.

4 tbsp (60 ml) pina colada mix
  or coconut milk
3/4 cup (175 ml) pineapple
  juice
4 fresh strawberries
1/2 cup (125 ml) crushed ice
Sugar and fresh strawberries,
  for garnish

Pour colada mix or coconut milk in blender, add pineapple juice, fresh strawberries and crushed iced. Blend until smooth.

Serve in a glass rimmed with sugar and garnish with a fresh strawberry.

serves 1 medium-sized goblet

QUATTRINI

QUATTRO AT WHISTLER, WHISTLER, BC

A twist on perhaps the most famous cocktail of all, this quattrini is elegant enough for a special dinner, or double the ingredients and serve as a refreshing luncheon drink.

2 tbsp (30 ml) fruit punch
4 tbsp (60 ml) mineral water
3 tbsp (45 ml) cranberry juice
3 tbsp (45 ml) oz orange juice
Splash lime cordial
1 slice orange, for garnish

In cocktail shaker with plenty of ice, combine fruit punch, mineral water, cranberry and orange juices and lime cordial. Shake, strain and serve.

serves 1 martini glass

TRADEWINDS

FERN RESORT, ORILLIA, ON

A hint of grenadine adds just the right sweet touch to this colourful citrus drink.

1/2 cup (125 ml) grapefruit juice
1/2 cup (125 ml) orange juice
1 tsp (5 ml) grenadine
4 tbsp (60 ml) soda water

Pour grapefruit juice, orange juice and grenadine in cocktail shaker (or glass jar with lid) and shake vigorously for 10 seconds. Pour into glass and top with soda water.

serves 1 wine glass

Left: Quattrini

WHITE CHOCOLATE NON-MARTINI

LA PERLA, DARTMOUTH, NS

Chef James MacDougall calls this a "nice dessert drink anytime of the year. Passion fruit is festive as well as seductive and refreshing."

1/2 cup (125 ml) whipping cream
1 cup (250 ml) white chocolate, finely chopped
3/4 cup (175 ml) passion fruit juice or puree
1/4 cup (50 ml) simple syrup (see p. 37)
1/2 cup (125) half and half (blend) cream
white chocolate shavings, for garnish

Bring whipping cream to boil, add chocolate and remove from heat, stirring to melt. Let cool. In cocktail shaker, combine passion fruit juice, syrup and blend. Shake with ice and pour into chocolate cream mixture. Sprinkle with white chocolate shavings and serve in martini glasses.

serves 6 martini glasses

Right: White Chocolate Non-Martini

Sips of Sunshine

Fruit and Veggies from the Juice Bar

The fruits of summer are packed with flavour. Blend them together, serve on ice and you have vitamins galore. But berries are just the beginning when you can cool down with cucumbers, carrots and celery, blended into healthy beverages.

Left: Raspberry Vinegar

RASPBERRY VINEGAR

There's nothing quite like a shot or two of raspberry vinegar, made with fresh berries, to liven up a glass of water.

4 cups (1 L) red wine vinegar
24 cups (6 L) raspberries
sugar

Pour vinegar over half the berries, and let stand 6 to 8 hours or overnight. Strain through cheesecloth onto the other half of berries, and let stand another 6 to 8 hours. Strain again. For each cup of liquid, add 1/4 cup (50 ml) sugar and boil for 20 minutes.

Use the vinegar to flavour water or soda water, 2 tbsp (30 ml) per 8 oz glass.

Serve in tall, frosted glasses over ice cubes. For a special touch, freeze a raspberry in each cube.

If you're planning on keeping raspberry vinegar a while, you may either freeze it in small containers or bottle it following manufacturer's instructions on your canner.

APPLE BLOSSOM TIME

L'EMOTION RESTAURANT, WEST VANCOUVER, BC

This is a drink from Finland — but with our profusion of fresh local apples on both coasts, it could just have easily originated in Canada.

3 cups (750 ml) apple cider, non-alcoholized
1 1/2 cups (375 ml) apple juice
1 cup (250 ml) apricot nectar or apricot juice

Pour apple cider, apple juice and apricot nectar into large container or punch bowl. Stir and serve over ice.

serves 6 tall glasses

FRESH GRAPE JUICE

If you're fortunate enough to have grapes growing in your backyard or accessible through a local vineyard, there's nothing quite like fresh grape juice.

16 cups (4 L) green or purple grapes
1 tbsp (15ml) fresh lemon juice

In blender, blend grapes and lemon juice until very smooth, about 1 minute. Pour mixture through sieve into bowl, pressing hard to squeeze out all liquids. Juice will keep refrigerated for a couple of days, but it's best drunk when fresh.

serves 2 juice glasses

Right: Fresh Grape Juice

EXTRAORDINARY TOMATO-FENNEL JUICE

The fennel leaves a distinct licorice undertone that takes this tomato juice out of the realm of the ordinary.

4 large tomatoes, quartered
1 small fennel bulb, chopped
2 celery ribs with leaves, chopped
1 cup (250 ml) loosely packed fresh flat-leaf
  parsley sprigs, chopped
2 tsp (10 ml) salt

In food processor, finely chop tomatoes, fennel, celery and parsley. Let stand covered in large bowl at room temperature for 90 minutes.

Line large sieve with cheesecloth and set over large glass bowl. Carefully pour tomato mixture into centre of cheesecloth, then gather up edges of cheesecloth to form a large sack and, working over sieve, squeeze solids to extract as much juice as possible. Discard solids.

Chill juice until cold, about 1 hour, and stir in salt before serving.

serves 4 juice glasses

RUNDLES SUMMER FRESH TOMATO JUICE

RUNDLES, STRATFORD, ON

4 to 5 lbs (1.5 kg) tomatoes (choose only red,
*   ripe and juicy tomatoes)*
1 to 2 cups (250 - 500 ml) water
salt and pepper, to taste

Remove any bruises and blemishes, and cut
tomatoes in half. Put in large stainless-steel pan.

Add 1 to 2 cups water to the tomatoes, cover
and bring to a boil. Reduce heat and simmer on
very low for around 30 minutes. Once the
tomatoes are soft and slightly cooked, pour into
a food mill, forcing as much pulp as possible
through the mill, then season with salt and
pepper to taste.

serves 4 juice glasses

A food mill is a useful tool for separating skin, seeds
and fibrous pulp from juice of fruits, such as
tomatoes, grapes, currants and gooseberries.

COOL AS A CUCUMBER

The lightness of cucumber and the fresh mint taste will cool you down quickly on a hot summer day.

8 seedless (English) cucumbers, peeled
2 cups (500 ml) water
1 tbsp (15 ml) chopped fresh mint

Purée cucumbers, mint and ice cubes in a blender; add water and stir.

Serve chilled with sprig of fresh mint or orange twist in a tall glass.

serves 2 tall glasses

HYDRATOR

This fruit-veggie combination is a great thirst quencher and loaded with vitamins.

6 apples
4 celery stalks
4 oranges, peeled
pinch of fresh dill

Juice apples, celery stalks, and oranges together in juicer.

Serve chilled with celery stalk for garnish and sprinkled with fresh dill.

serves 2 medium glasses

CARROT COOLER

Vegetable juice is quick and nutritious. Start with this good basic recipe and feel free to improvise with almost any fresh vegetables.

6 carrots
2 apples
1 tbsp (15 ml) chopped cilantro
1 tsp (5 ml) lime juice

Put carrots and apples through juicer. Add cilantro and lime juice and stir well with a whisk.

Serve with a splash of hot sauce for extra zing!

serves 1 juice glass

Cool Cuppa

Iced Tea and Coffee

Seated on a verandah swing, sipping iced tea — what a perfect way to relax and watch the neighbourhood wind down on a summer's evening. Iced tea and coffee can be made in the morning and chilled throughout the day.

Left: Herbal Iced Tea

CHAI STORM

PRAIRIE INK RESTAURANT, WINNIPEG, MANITOBA

This chai tea chiller has that aromatic hint of Indian spices.

1/2 cup (125 ml) strained chai tea
2 tbsp (30 ml) chocolate syrup
2 cups (500 ml) ice
1 cup (250 ml) skim milk

Put all ingredients into a blender. Mix just till blended, about 1 minute. Serve in glass mugs with a sprinkle of ground cinnamon, or with a cinnamon stick in each mug.

For a sweeter and richer Chai Storm, substitute 1 cup of vanilla ice cream or gelati for ice and skim milk.

serves 2 tall glasses

CHAI TEA

Hot or cold, chai tea is delicious, but hot tea is popular in India, even in summer time, for cooling down the body!

4 cups (1 L) water
4 tea bags
1/2 tsp (2 ml) crushed ginger root
1 medium cinnamon stick
1/4 tsp (1 ml) fennel seeds (optional)
1/4 tsp (1 ml) dried cardamom (optional)
2 to 3 tsp (10-15 ml) sugar or honey (more to taste)
1 1/2 cups (375 ml) whole milk

In large saucepan, bring water to boil. Add tea bags, ginger, cinnamon, fennel and cardamom. Let simmer 3 to 4 minutes, covered. Add milk and return to boil. Stir in honey or sugar. Strain and enjoy.

serves 4 cups

Right: Chai Tea

VELOCITY

PRAIRIE INK RESTAURANT, WINNIPEG, MANITOBA

This vanilla coffee is an intense wake-up on a summer's morning.

2 shots (100 ml) espresso
1 1/2 tbsp (25 ml) vanilla syrup or 1/2 tsp
  (2 ml) vanilla extract plus 1 tsp (5 ml) sugar
1/4 cup (50 ml) skim milk
1/2 cup (125 ml) vanilla ice cream

Blend all ingredients together in a drink mixer. Serve at once in a tall glass. Garnish with vanilla beans scraped from a fresh vanilla pod, or sprinkle with chocolate shavings.

serves 1 tall glass

ICED PEPPERMINT PATTIE

GABRIEAU'S BISTRO, ANTIGONISH, NS

The peppermint in this iced coffee will take your breath away and instantly turn down the heat a few degrees — and it's sweet enough for dessert on its own.

1 cup (250 ml) crushed ice
2 tbsp (30 ml) hot espresso or strong instant
  coffee
1 tbsp (15 ml) chocolate syrup
2 tbsp (30 ml) chocolate mint syrup
1/4 tsp (1 ml) peppermint extract
1 tbsp (15 ml) half and half (blend) cream

In blender, combine crushed ice, coffee, chocolate and chocolate mint syrup, peppermint extract and blend. Process for 20 seconds.

serves 1 tall glass

Right: Iced Peppermint Pattie

HERBAL ICED TEA

LION INN, LUNENBURG, NS

This herbal tea has the flavouring built right into the tea bag — and no caffeine. Try different combinations of flavoured herbal teas to create your own special drink.

4 cups (1 L) water
2 lemon zinger tea bags
3 raspberry tea bags

In large pot, bring water to boil. Add tea bags and steep for 15 minutes. Strain into container, refrigerate and serve chilled.

serves 4 tall glasses

Left: Herbal Iced Tea

LEMON MINT ICED TEA

LA PERLA, DARTMOUTH, NS

Lemon and mint are classic companions to iced tea, and together they make this summertime staple even better.

8 tea bags
8 cups (2 L) cold water
1 cup (250 ml) fresh lemon mint, chopped
sugar to taste

Combine tea bags, water and lemon mint into a clear glass container. Seal tightly and place container on window ledge or other sunny location. Sun brew tea all day. After tea has brewed, chill and serve, adding sugar if desired.

serves 8 tall glasses

ICED COFFEE THAI STYLE

Traditional Thai iced coffee is made double-strength and then sweetened with condensed milk. This version is less intense than its origins – not quite as sweet and not quite as strong.

4 tsp (20 ml) dark roast coffee, ground
2 tsp (10 ml) ground cardamom
4 tbsp (60 ml) sugar
4 tbsp (60 ml) coffee cream (18% m.f.)
1 tsp (5 ml) almond extract
Crushed ice
Cinnamon sticks, for garnish

Add cardamom to coffee and place in coffee maker. When coffee is brewed, stir in sugar and let dissolve, then leave to cool. Stir in coffee cream and almond extract.

Half fill four highball glasses with crushed ice. Pour in coffee. Garnish with cinnamon sticks.

serves 4 highball glasses

HANNAH'S ICED MOCHACHINO

This blend of coffee and chocolate can be adjusted to suite either chocoholics or coffee aficionados.

2 cups brewed coffee,
1 tsp (5 ml) brown sugar
1 large pinch ground cinnamon
2 tbsp (30 ml) chocolate syrup
2 tbsp (30 ml) coffee cream (18% m.f.)

When coffee is still warm stir in sugar, cinnamon and chocolate syrup. Let cool, stir in cream. Half fill two medium glasses with crushed ice and add mochachino.

Garnish with a sprinkle of cinnamon or cocoa powder.

serves 2 medium glasses

SUN TEA

ARBOR VIEW INN, LUNENBURG, NS

This method of letting the sun brew the tea is traditional in the American South.

4 cups (1 L) cold water
5 tea bags (orange pekoe)
sugar (optional)

Pour water into quart-size clear glass container, then add tea bags. Seal tightly. Place container on window ledge or other sunny location. Let sun brew tea for 4 to 5 hours. After tea has brewed, chill and serve, adding sugar if desired.

serves 4 tall glasses

Left: Sun Tea

RUSSIAN TEA

DUNDEE ARMS INN, MABOU, NS

Since the mid-1700s, Russians have enjoyed tea from samovars, large urns that keep the tea heated all day. You may not have such an urn on hand, but this delightfully fragrant tea will taste just as good prepared in a large tea pot and then cooled.

8 cups (2 L) water
1 1/4 cups (300 ml) sugar
4 large oranges, juiced (about 2 cups, about 500 ml)
1 lemon, juiced (about 3 tbsp, about 45 ml)
1 1/2 tbsp (25 ml) orange zest
2 tsp (10 ml) lemon zest
8 whole cloves
5 tsp (25 ml) tea leaves

In large pot, bring water to boil. Stir in sugar, orange and lemon juices, orange and lemon zests and cloves. Pour over tea leaves, steep 5 minutes. Strain and cool. Serve chilled.

serves 8 tall glasses

Blender Bliss

Smoothies and Lassies

Thick, rich, satisfying — with a smoothie you enjoy the health benefits of a meal and the taste sensation of a sinful shake. You can adapt the sinful side by substituting low-fat yogurt for ice cream and using low-fat milk. The traditional fruit smoothie needs little introduction, but a cucumber smoothie breaks new ground.

CANTALOUPE SMOOTHIE

DIVA AT THE MET, VANCOUVER, BC

Serve this smoothie in a martini glass for an elegant after dinner refresher, or double up the fruit content and use it to get a jump-start on your day.

2 cups (500 ml) diced cantaloupe (about one small melon)
1 cup (250 ml) plain yogurt
1/2 cup (125 ml) organic apple juice
2 melon balls, scooped from cantaloupe, for garnish

Add cantaloupe, yogurt and apple juice to blender, process until smooth.

Serve in chilled martini glass, and garnish with melon ball.

serves 2 goblets

Right: Cantaloupe Smoothie

CUCUMBER SMOOTHIE

DUFFERIN INN, SAINT JOHN, NB

And now for something completely different: this elegant drink begs to be served at dinner. Its subtle flavours are accentuated with a splash of Tabasco and lime — a true smoothie for adults!

1 large seedless (English) cucumber, peeled and chopped
1 cup (250 ml) plain yogurt (or sour cream if you prefer a thicker, tangier smoothie)
1 tsp (5 ml) lime juice
1/4 tsp (1 ml) green Tabasco
1/4 tsp (1 ml) salt
1/4 tsp (1ml) white pepper
1/3 cup (75 ml) fresh dill
1 cup (250 ml) ice cubes
1/2 to 1 cup (125 to 250 ml) mineral water

In blender, add cucumber, yogurt, lime juice, Tabasco, salt, pepper, dill and ice cubes. Process until smooth. Add mineral water to desired consistency, stir and serve.

serves 2 large glasses

LASSI

Lassi is a traditional South Asian drink made from a buttermilk or yogurt base, often thinned with rosewater. It is delicious plain, or with mango.

1 cup (250 ml) yogurt
1 cup (250 ml) cold water
2 tsp (10 ml) sugar
pinch of cinnamon or a few drops rosewater

Place all ingredients in blender or drink mixer and process 10 to 15 seconds.

serves 2 tall glasses

Left: Cucumber Smoothie

YOGURT BANANA LASSI WITH SAFFRON

CASINO NOVA SCOTIA AND HOTEL, HALIFAX, NS

This variation of the traditional drink of India has a sunny yellow colour from the addition of saffron.

1 pinch saffron
1/2 cup (125 ml) water
2 cups (500 ml) yogurt
2 ripe bananas
4 tbsp (60 ml) honey
1/2 cup (125 ml) crushed ice or 4 ice cubes

In a saucepan boil saffron with water for 3-4 minutes. Set in refrigerator to cool. Once cool, process saffron water in blender with yogurt, bananas, honey and ice cubes. Serve this refreshing drink in iced-tea glasses with a slice of orange and lemon for garnish.

serves 2 tall glasses

FRUIT SMOOTHIE

OLD HOUSE RESTAURANT, COURTENAY, BC

This is a great way to start the morning. If you prefer your smoothies thicker, add yogurt.

2 cups fresh orange or cranberry juice
1 medium banana
2 cups berries (strawberries, blueberries or raspberries)

Put fruit juice, banana and berries in blender and process until smooth. Pour and enjoy!

serves 2 large glasses

Right: Fruit Smoothie

Fun and Festive

Dressed-up Drinks for all Ages

With names like Jungle Juice, Shakin' Jamaican and Lava Flow, these cool summer treats are fresh and imaginative. For a summer celebration with a splash of colour, these drinks will steal the show if you dress them up in funky glassware and tempting garnishes.

Left: Lava Flow

SHAKIN' JAMAICAN

SALTY'S BEACH HOUSE RESTAURANT, PENTICTON, BC

Definitely a beach party drink, a fun name like this needs a fun presentation to match. A brightly coloured umbrella and a cocktail pick with a couple of cherries will do.

1/2 cup (125 ml) pineapple juice
1/4 cup (50 ml) milk
1 tsp (5 ml) coconut syrup
6 whole strawberries
1/4 cup (50 ml) crushed ice

In blender, process pineapple juice, milk, coconut syrup, strawberries and ice until smooth. Serve chilled.

serves 1 tall tumbler

Left: Shakin' Jamaican

There are many kinds of mint, including spearmint, peppermint and lemon mint. Each one has its distinct aroma. Most are very easy to cultivate, so you can have fresh mint all summer and fall.

MINT SPRITZER

CHANTERELLE COUNTRY INN, NORTH RIVER,
ST. ANNS BAY, NS

"It was always a special occasion in our house when my mother made this" recalls Earlene Busch of Chanterelle Country Inn, "especially in the middle of a hot summer." This invigorating spritzer is sure to become a special occasion for you, too.

2 cups (500 ml) fresh mint leaves
1 cup (250 ml) boiling water
1 cup (250 ml) cold water
1 cup (250 ml) sugar
6 tbsp (90 ml) lemon juice
2 cups (500 ml) orange juice
pinch of powdered ginger
ginger ale
mint leaves, to garnish

Pick stems from mint, gently crush leaves and place in bowl. Pour bowling water over mint and let steep for 20 to 30 minutes. Strain and reserve liquid.

In medium saucepan, heat cold water and stir in sugar until dissolved. Add lemon and orange juices and powdered ginger.

Combine mint liquid with juice mixture and chill. Just before serving, add 2 parts ginger ale to 1 part combined mint-juice mixture.

Serve in glass, rimmed with sugar and garnish with fresh mint leaves.

serves 12 goblets

Left: Mint Spritzer

WHISTLER WHISTLE WETTER

EDGEWATER LODGE, WHISTLER, BC

This colourful concoction is as fun to drink as it is to pronounce.

1/2 cup (125 ml) lemonade
1/2 cup (125 ml) cranberry juice
dash of grenadine
3 to 4 ice cubes
1 lemon slice, for garnish

Pour lemonade, cranberry juice and grenadine in cocktail shaker. Add ice cubes and shake, strain into glass.

serves 1 medium-sized goblet

BORA-BORA

TEAHOUSE RESTAURANT IN STANLEY PARK, VANCOUVER, BC

This is a wonderfully refreshing and exotic drink, reminiscent of long warm evenings on a Polynesian Isle.

1/3 cup.(75 ml) pineapple juice
3 tbsp (45 ml) passion fruit juice
1 1/2 tsp (7 ml) lemon juice
1 1/2 tsp (7 ml) grenadine

In large glass, stir together pineapple, passion fruit and lemon juices and grenadine. Add ice cubes and enjoy.

serves 1 tall glass

JUNGLE JUICE

THE OLD HOUSE RESTAURANT, COURTENAY, BC

Great for kids' parties, serve this cool concoction
with fancy straws and cocktail umbrellas.

1/2 cup (125 ml) lime juice
1 cup (250 ml) orange juice
1 cup 250 ml) pineapple juice
1 cup 250 ml) cranberry juice

Combine lime, orange, pineapple and cranberry
juices. Stir together and serve with ice.

**serves 4 tall
glasses**

BUBBLING JADE PUNCH

TEAHOUSE RESTAURANT, VANCOUVER, BC

Once you've made this punch, you'll see where the name comes from. It's great for kids' parties but if you want a more "grown-up" drink, just skip the Jell-O.

2 packages (85 g each) of lime Jell-O
2 cups (500 ml) boiling water
4 cups (1 L) cold water
1 can (355 ml) of frozen lemonade concentrate,
    thawed and undiluted
2 cups (500 ml) pineapple juice
8 cups (2 L) ginger ale

In large bowl, dissolve gelatin in boiling water. Stir in cold water, lemonade concentrate and pineapple juice. Chill well, but no longer than an hour or so the gelatin will not set. Stir in ginger ale just before serving.

serves 36 punch cups

BLUSHING BRIDE

AERIE RESORT, MALAHAT, BC

Refreshing and smooth, this soft- pink blend has innocence and lightness, like its namesake.

3/4 cup (175 ml) pineapple juice
1 1/2 tbsp (25 ml) coffee cream (17%)
dash of grenadine

In cocktail shaker, mix pineapple juice, cream and grenadine. Pour and serve.

serves 1 champagne flute

Left: Blushing Bride

CHEAPSIDE MAPLE-PEAR NECTAR

CHEAPSIDE CAFÉ, HALIFAX, NS

This delicious nectar has that quintessential Canadian ingredient — maple syrup. Just a small amount is enough to add a smooth sweetness to this drink, perfect for a summer picnic.

1 1/2 cups (375 ml) pear juice
1 1/2 cups (375 ml) mineral water
1 tbsp (15 ml) maple syrup
1 tsp (5 ml) lemon juice

Combine pear juice, mineral water, maple syrup and lemon juice in pitcher. Stir and serve.

serves 4 medium-sized goblets

Make fresh pear juice in an electric juicer or a blender. Peel, core and dice the pears. Blend until smooth with a little water or apple juice to keep the blade from clogging.

Right: Cheapside Maple-Pear Nectar

LAVA FLOW

TEAHOUSE RESTAURANT IN
STANLEY PARK, VANCOUVER,
BC

At once exotic and fun, this
makes a great party drink.

1/2 cup (125 ml) 10% cream
1/2 cup (125 ml) pineapple
* juice*
1 tbsp (15 ml) coconut milk
1/2 banana
1/2 cup (125 ml) fresh
* strawberries*

In blender, add cream,
pineapple juice, coconut milk,
banana and strawberries. Purée
until smooth, serve chilled.

You can serve this in a
hollowed-out coconut half,
with a big umbrella and straw.

serves 1 large glass

SUNRISER

ACTON'S GRILL AND CAFÉ, WOLFVILLE, NS

The name and bright colours would make this a
great brunch beverage.

1/4 cup (50 ml) crushed ice
1 tsp (5 ml) grenadine
1/2 cup (125 ml) pineapple juice
1/2 cup (125 ml) orange juice
cherry, for garnish

Put ice in goblet; add grenadine, then pineapple
and orange juices. Do not stir before serving.
Garnish with cherry on a cocktail pick.

serves 1 medium-sized wine glass

Creamy Cool

Malts, Sorbets and Shakes

There are times when real dessert is just too much of a good thing but something cold and creamy seems just right. From the tangy Sorbetto al Limone to the intensity of Double Blueberry Malt, these recipes are beyond temptation.

Left: Double Blueberry Malt

DOUBLE BLUEBERRY MALT

BARTLETT LODGE, ALGONQUIN PARK, ON

You can make this delicious shake without the malted milk powder if you have trouble finding it; although it won't have quite the same old-fashioned soda fountain flavour it will still be well worth the effort.

3/4 cup (175 ml) fresh blueberries
1/4 cup (50 ml) whole milk
1/4 cup (50 ml) malted milk powder
1 tbsp (15 ml) sugar
1 cup (250 ml) vanilla ice cream
2 small scoops blueberry sorbet and 8 whole
  blueberries, for garnish

In blender, combine berries, milk, malted milk powder, sugar and ice cream. Blend until smooth.

Pour malt into fluted soda fountain glass, top with sorbet and garnish with berries.

serves 2 large glasses

BERRY BLAST

OPA!, HALIFAX, NS

A real favorite with kids, this sweet and filling smoothie makes for a scrumptious after dinner treat.

1 cup (250 ml) fresh blueberries or strawberries
1 banana
1 cup (250 ml) orange juice
1/2 cup (125 ml) whipping cream
1 tbsp (15 ml) sugar

In blender, combine berries, banana, orange juice, whipping cream and sugar. Process until smooth and serve.

serves 2 large glasses

Right: Berry Blast

An alternative to a blender is a drink or milkshake mixer. These usually come with a detachable stainless-steel cup in which to put the ingredients, and an integral blending arm with which to mix everything. These work great for soft ingredients and liquids. They make your favourite shake into a foamy sensation.

BANANA DREAMSICLE

FERN RESORT, ORILLIA, ON

This nutrition-packed smoothie makes for a particularly healthy and refreshing end — or start — to an adventure-packed summer's day.

1 cup (250 ml) orange juice
1 cup (250 ml) pineapple juice
2 medium bananas
1/2 cup (125 ml) crushed ice
2 fresh pineapple rings, for garnish

Pour orange and pineapple juices into blender, add banana and process until smooth. Add crushed ice, process 10 to 20 seconds.

Pour into glasses and garnish with pineapple rings on rim of glass.

serves 2 large glasses

CHOCOLATE MONKEY

FERN RESORT, ORILLIA ON

Fun to make and fun to drink, this is a substitute for dessert.

4 scoops chocolate ice cream
2 cups (500 ml) chocolate milk
1 medium banana
1/2 cup (125 ml) crushed ice
1 cup (250 ml) chocolate sauce and 1
  banana, for garnish

Put ice cream, chocolate milk and banana in blender and process until smooth. Add crushed iced and process 10 to 20 seconds more.

Line inside of a soda fountain glass with chocolate: pour chocolate sauce into measuring cup. Hold glass in one hand at a 45-degree angle, and chocolate sauce in the other. Put the spout of the measuring cup to the rim of the glass and pour the chocolate syrup slowly while you twist the glass. You should end up with a chocolate-lined glass. Garnish with the other half of the banana, sliced. Add a big straw and you're all set!

serves 2 large glasses

SORBETTO AL LIMONE

LA PERLA , DARTMOUTH, NS

An elegant encore to a summer evening meal,
this drink is both a beverage and a dessert.

1/2 cup (125 ml) lemon sorbet
2 lemons, juiced (about 6 tbsp)
1/2 cup (125 ml) heavy cream
1 cup (250 ml) de-alcoholized sparkling white
  wine
strawberry or fruit skewers, for garnish

In blender, combine lemon sorbet, lemon juice
and heavy cream and purée. Add wine and stir.

Pour into champagne flute and garnish with
strawberry or fruit skewer.

serves 2 champagne flutes

BANANA RASPBERRY MILKSHAKE

WESTOVER INN, ST. MARYS, ON

Ruth Moxley created this on an especially hot day for the housekeepers at the Westover Inn. "They work so hard," she says, "they deserve a treat!" And so do you.

3/4 cup (175 ml) vanilla ice cream (approx 2 large scoops)
3/4 cup (175 ml) 2% milk
1/2 cup (125 ml) fresh raspberries
1 medium banana
1/2 tsp (2 ml) vanilla extract

Purée ice cream, milk, raspberries, banana and vanilla extra in blender until smooth. Pour into soda fountain or smoothie glasses, and don't forget your straw!

serves 2 large glasses

Index